Table of Contents

Take A Trip Around Southern Recipes

Around Southern Africa with 30 Unique Recipes

BY: Ida Smith

License Notes

Introduction

How often do you crave Southern African cuisines? Do you wish to travel down there for a vacation to satisfy your cravings? Well, with the pandemic and various countries being extremely careful, traveling has become a bit difficult. What's more challenging is the world economy that is affecting a lot of people. You don't have to worry too much, and this cookbook has brought your favorite Southern African dish to your doorstep. You don't need to travel anymore. Enjoy preparing each meal with our unique recipes from the comfort of your home.

Recipe 1 - South African Styled Yellow Rice

This is a fantastic traditional Southern recipe that came from Cape Malays. It is easy to prepare and can be eaten with any meat of your choice.

Prep time: 45 minutes

Serves: 6

Recipes

- 1 cup of white rice, long grain
- 1/2 teaspoon of salt
- 2 teaspoons of ground turmeric
- 1/2 cup of white sugar
- 1/2 teaspoon of ground cinnamon
- 1/2 cup of raisin
- 1 tablespoon of butter

Direction

Mix the rice, turmeric, salt, cinnamon, sugar, raisins, butter, and water in a pan and allow it to boil. After it boils, reduce the heat and let it simmer for about 30 minutes.

Remove, let it sit for a few minutes, then serve warm.

Recipe 2 - Spicy Southern African Styled Sausage

This recipe is simple and easy to prepare. It is one of the favorite snacks that are common in the south.

Prep time: 60 minutes

Serves: 4

Recipes

- 2 pounds of pork shoulder, boneless and chilled
- 1 pound of pork fat, fresh and chilled
- 2 teaspoons of salt
- 1 teaspoon of fresh ground black pepper
- 1 tablespoon of ground sage
- 1 teaspoon of red pepper flakes, dried
- 1/3 cup of cold water

Direction

Chop your pork and the pork fat, put it in a meat grinder, and blend smoothly. Add your remaining ingredients into the blender, mix properly and use your hands to knead the mixture until very smooth.

Wrap sausage in a plastic wrap and chill before serving.

Recipe 3 - Creamy Oyster and Almond Pie

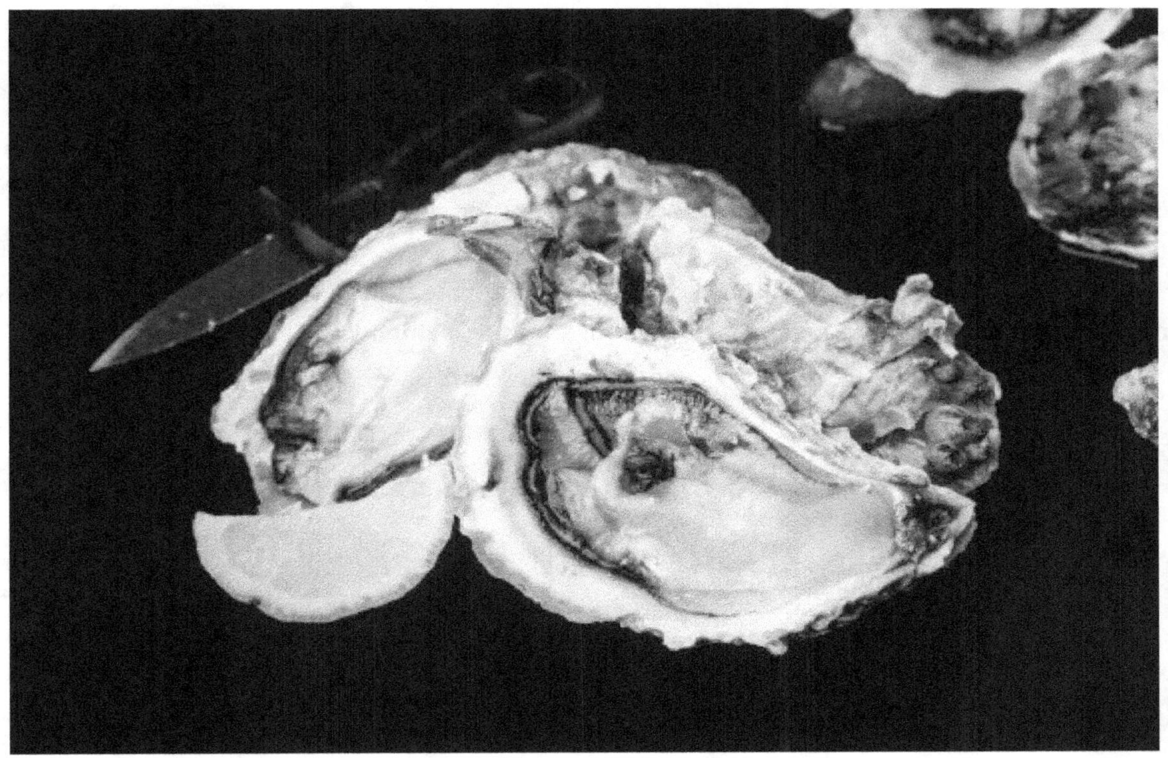

Looking for a nice snacks that has the southern taste? Then this unique apple pie recipe is one that you must try.

Prep time: 50 minutes

Serves: 6

Recipes

- 1/2 cup of almonds, silvered
- 2 cups of soda crackers, crushed
- 1/3 tablespoon of ground nutmeg
- 1 teaspoon of salt
- 1/2 teaspoon of cayenne pepper
- 1/2 cup of dried sherry
- 1 pound of fresh Oyster with liquor reserved

- 1 teaspoon of Worcestershire sauce
- 1/2 stick of butter, chopped
- 1 cup of half and half

Direction

Preheat your oven to about 300°F. Spread your almonds on the baking sheet, put in your oven, and bake for about 15 minutes or until it is brown, turning it severally and set aside.

Mix the crackers, salt, cayenne pepper, and nutmeg in a bowl and set aside. Then in another goal, mix the Worcestershire sauce, sherry, and oyster liquor in another bowl. In your baking pan, arrange the oysters and crackers and sprinkle the liquor mixture on it.

Place butter on every layer, then add the half and half around, put in your oven, and bake for about 20 minutes. Spread the almonds on it, bake again for another 10 minutes.

Remove from oven and serve hot.

Recipe 4 - Mashed Potatoes and Buttermilk

This might seem like a lot of work, and you may prefer to just order it from a nice restaurant. But you certainly not enjoy it like the one you will prepare yourself.

Prep time: 45 minutes
Serves: 5
Recipes

- 5 peeled and chopped russet potatoes
- 4 tablespoons of chopped softened butter
- 2 tablespoons of horseradish
- 1/3 tablespoon of salt
- 1/2 teaspoon of fresh ground black pepper

Direction

Place your potatoes in a pan, add water and boil until it is tender. Remove from pan, drain and transfer to another pan. Reduce heat, add butter to the pan, and mash with your electric mixer.

When smooth, add your remaining ingredients, keep mixing until your potato is fluffy and very light. Transfer to a serving plate and enjoy.

Recipe 5 - Brown Rice and Mushroom

Brown rice is very nutritious, and the flavor is exceptional. This meal is more remarkable because it is prepared with mushrooms, and it is one meal of the south that you need to try.

Prep time: 60 minutes
Serves: 4
Recipes

- 1 medium-sized well-diced onion
- 1 chopped celery rib
- 2 tablespoons of butter
- 2 cans of beef broth
- 1 cup of brown rice
- 1 cup of mushroom, chopped
- 1 teaspoon of salt

- 1 teaspoon of fresh ground black pepper

Direction

Put your celery, butter, onion, and beef broth in a pan and let it boil. Then add the rice slowly while stirring, reduce heat, cover and allow it to simmer for about 30 minutes.

Add your mushrooms, salt, and pepper and continue cooking for another 20 minutes or until the liquid is absorbed and your rice soft.

Remove from heat and serve hot.

Recipe 6 - Rice and Pecan

Do you need a quick Southern meal to complement your roasted chicken? Then this tasty pecan rice is easy to make and delicious and a suitable complementary dish.

Prep time: 20 minutes

Serves: 4

Recipes

- 3 tablespoons of butter
- 1 small-sized onion, diced
- 1/3 cup of fresh parsley leaves, chopped
- 2 tablespoons of pimento, well chopped
- 2 cups of long-grain rice
- 1 teaspoon of salt
- 1/2 teaspoon of fresh black ground pepper
- 2 cups of chicken broth
- 1 tablespoon of toasted pecans, crushed

Direction

Melt butter in a pan, add onions, and let it simmer for about 5 minutes. Add your pimentos, salt, and parsley, stir and let it simmer for another few minutes. Add your rice and stir properly while it simmers for another 2 minutes.

Add your chicken broth and bring to boil until the liquid is absorbed and your rice is soft.

Remove from heat, let it relax for a few minutes, and serve hot with your pecans scattered on it.

Recipe 7 - Spicy Egg and Salmon

Are you looking for a perfect Southern Africa breakfast for your family? Then the spicy salmon and egg is your best choice. It is easy to prepare, and it is incredible.

Prep time: 20 minutes
Serves: 4
Recipes

- 1 pound of salmon fillet
- 3 tablespoons of oil
- 1/2 tablespoon of salt
- 1 tablespoon of smoked paprika
- 1 teaspoon of granules garlic
- 1 teaspoon of basil, dried
- 1/3 teaspoon of cayenne pepper

- 2 boiled eggs
- 4 cups of baby green
- 2 tablespoons of oil
- 1 tablespoon of lemon juice

Direction

Mix the salt, paprika, garlic, basil, and cayenne, and rub the mixture on the salmon. Heat oil in a pan, deep your salmon into the oil, and fry for about 5 minutes, turning each side.

Remove from heat and serve with baby greens, lemon juice, and eggs.

Recipe 8 - Nutmeg Seasoned Long Grain Rice with Nuts

The Southern Africans love good food, and this happens to be one of those favorite meals that have been in existence for years, and it can be served with any meat of your choice.

Prep time: 40 minutes

Serves: 4

Recipes

- 2 cups of chicken broth
- 2 cups of water
- 1/2 stick of butter
- 1/2 tablespoon of salt
- 2 cups of long-grain rice
- 1/2 cup of pine nuts
- 2 tablespoons of pistachio nuts, shelled

- 1/3 tablespoon of nutmeg

Direction

Pour your chicken broth into a large pan, add your water, part of your butter, and a little salt, and allow it to boil. Add your rice, cover the pan and let it boil on low heat until the rice is soft, and all liquid absorbed.

Melt your butter in another pan, add your nits and simmer until it becomes golden brown and stir while cooking. Remove your rice from heat, use a fork to fluff it, transfer to a serving bowl.

Add your nutmeg and nuts, mix properly and serve hot.

Recipe 9 - Cheesy Mushroom Steaks

Do you want to have a no-meat day? Then this is the perfect meal to eat without overthinking about it.

Prep time: 20 minutes

Serves: 4

Recipes

- 6 large mushrooms
- 1 cup of soy sauce
- 1 teaspoon of Maldon salt
- 1 tablespoon of oil
- 1 tablespoon of well-diced garlic
- 1/2 cup of feta cheese
- 1 tablespoon of fresh chives, chopped
- 1 teaspoon of fresh black ground pepper.

Direction

Rinse the mushroom and remove the stems, then dry. Mix the soy sauce, salt, oil, and garlic in a bowl. Drop the mushroom into the sauce mixture for about 20 minutes.

Heat the grill, brush with oil, remove mushroom from marinade, shake off excess marinade, place on the rack, grill for about 5 minutes, and turn the other side.

Remove from heat and serve. Sprinkle your feta cheese, chives, and black pepper.

Recipe 10 - Spicy Shrimp and Oyster

This meal can be traced back to the south, even though regions like Florida have claimed it. The meal is exotic, and it is made with rice.

Prep time: 40 minutes

Serves: 3

Recipes

- 4 bacon slices, diced
- 2 big onions, well diced
- 2 cups of rice
- 2 cups of chicken broth
- 3 well-chopped bell tomatoes
- 1 jar of pimentos drained and chopped
- 1 tablespoon of Worcestershire sauce

- 1/2 tablespoon of nutmeg
- 1 bay leaf
- 1/2 teaspoon of salt
- 1/2 teaspoon of ground black pepper
- 1/3 tablespoon of cayenne pepper
- 1 pound of fresh labeled and deveined shrimp
- 1 pint of oyster, fresh

Direction

Place your bacon in a big pan and fry until it becomes crispy. Remove and drain on paper towel and set aside. Pour out some of the fat and reserve a little in the pan. Add your onions, let it simmer while stirring for about 5 minutes or until it is sifted

Add your rice to the pan, stir properly and add your chicken broth, pimento, tomatoes, Worcestershire, bay leaf, nutmeg, salt, cayenne, and black pepper.

Stir together, cover it and let it cook for about 10 minutes. Then add your bacon, shrimp, and oyster, mix well, cover and cook until the water has been absorbed and your tender.

Remove from heat and serve hot.

Recipe 11 - Creamy Tasty Pancakes

Pancake can be considered as a quick and occasional snack that everyone loves. It also happens to be one of their easy and fast-making snacks.

Prep time: 30 minutes

Serves: 4

Recipes

- 2 cups of flour
- 1 tablespoon of baking powder
- 1 cup of full cream milk
- 1 cup of water
- 1 tablespoon of lemon juice
- 1/2 cup of oil
- 1/3 cup of cinnamon sugar

Direction

Sift your flour, salt, and baking powder into a bowl. Whisk your eggs, add milk, water, oil, and lemon juice, mix properly and pour the mixture into your flour. Mix properly until it is smooth.

Heat a little oil in a pan, spoon your pancake mixture into the hot oil and simmer for a few minutes on both sides. Remove and repeat the same procedure until the batter is finished.

Remove from heat and serve warm.

Recipe 12 - Rice Mold and Salmon

Rice is one of the significant foods the Southern Africans enjoy, and you could use it to bind various concoctions instead of bread crumbs. This is one of those kinds of meals that you can never miss.

Prep time: 60 minutes

Serves: 4

Recipes

- 3 cans of salmon, drained, skin and bone removed, and flaked
- 3 cups of rice, cooked
- 2 cups of milk
- 4 big eggs, whisked
- 2 tablespoons of melted butter
- 1 small-sized onion, diced
- 1/3 cup of green olives, chopped and stuffed with pimento

- 1/2 cup of parsley leaves, chopped
- 2 tablespoons of dill, chopped
- 2 tablespoons of lemon juice
- 1/2 teaspoon of salt
- 1/2 tablespoon of fresh ground black pepper.
- 1/2 cup of well-sliced cucumber
- 1/2 cup of paprika

Direction

Preheat your oven to about 400°F. Grease a fish mold with your butter, sprinkle the sides and bottom with paprika, and set aside. Mix all your ingredients in one bowl except for the cucumber.

Use your hands to ensure everything is properly mixed, transfer the mixture to the fish mold and bake for about 50 minutes. When it is firm, remove it from the oven and the fish mold, set it aside on a wire rack to drain off any liquid, and cool.

When it is cool, serve in a serving dish with your cucumber as garnishing.

Recipe 13 - Tasty Pumpkin Casserole

This is an amazing dish gotten from the South. It tastes heavenly, and it is very filling.

Prep time: 40 minutes

Serves: 3

Recipes

- 1/2 cup of sugar
- 1/2 cup of butter
- 3 big eggs, whisked
- 1 cup of pumpkin puree
- 1/2 cup of milk
- 1/2 cup of flour
- 1 tablespoon of baking powder
- 1/3 teaspoon of ground cinnamon.

Direction

Preheat your oven to about 400°F. Grease your baking pan and set it aside. Whisk your butter, sugar, eggs in a bowl, mix properly until it is smooth. Add your pumpkin, mix well.

Add your milk, flour, and baking powder to the pumpkin mixture, mix well until it is smooth. Pour mixture into your baking pan and bake for about 50 minutes.

Sprinkle the cinnamon on it, bake for another few minutes. Remove and serve hot.

Recipe 14 - Rice Casserole and Fried Onion

Do you need an effortless side dish? Then rice casserole is a fantastic Southern meal that you should try.

Prep time: 80 minutes

Serves: 5

Recipes

- 1/2 stick of butter
- 6 medium-sized Vidalia onions, diced
- 4 cups of water
- 1/2 tablespoon of salt
- 1 cup of rice
- 1 cup of Swiss cheese, grated
- 1 cup of half and half

- 1 teaspoon of fresh ground black pepper

Direction

Preheat your oven to about 300°F. Melt your butter in a large pan over medium heat. Add your onions, simmer and stir for about 10 minutes until it is soft. Remove from heat and set aside.

In another pan, put your water and salt and let it boil. Then add your rice and cool for about 5 minutes, remove from heat, and drain. Mix the onions, rice, half and half, cheese, and pepper in a large bowl and stir consistently.

Transfer mixture into a casserole pan, put it in your oven and bake until it is golden brown or for at least 60 minutes. Remove and serve hot.

Recipe 15 - Chicken in Chutney Sauce

This is also another one of South African's finest meals, and it is delicious. Mixing it with salad or rice makes it more filling.

Prep time: 50 minutes
Serves: 4
Recipes

- 10 chicken thighs
- 1 jar of chutney, hot
- 1 pack of onion soup mix, dry

Direction

Preheat your oven to about 360°F. Mix your chutney, onion mix, in a bowl and mix properly. Season your chicken with a little salt and pepper. Place chicken in a baking dish and pour the chutney mixture on it.

Place in the oven and cook until the sauce becomes brown.

Remove from oven and serve with anything on the side.

Recipe 16 - Okra and Tomato Stew

Here comes another popular southern dish that has been in existence for years, and it is still as tasty as it used to be.

Prep time: 25 minutes
Serves: 4
Recipes

- 4 bacon slices
- 1 big onion, diced
- 1 clove of garlic, minced
- 1 pound of fresh okra, stems and firm, chopped round
- 4 big ripe tomatoes, peeled and diced
- 1 small red pepper, seed removed and chopped
- 1 tablespoon of salt
- 1 teaspoon of fresh ground black pepper

- 1/3 teaspoon of thyme
- 1/2 teaspoon of dried basil
- 2 cups of cooked rice

Direction

Put your bacon in a pan and fry until it is crispy. Remove and drain with a paper towel and set aside. Remove fat from the pan and remain a little. Add your onions and garlic to the pan and simmer for about 5 minutes.

Add the tomatoes, okra, red pepper, thyme, black pepper, salt, and basil, cover the pan and let it cook until tender. Remove from pan and serve with your rice and bacon.

Recipe 17 - Beef in Curry Soup

This is one of South Africa's favorite meals that originated from the North, and it is a must-try meal.

Prep time: 1 hour 50 minutes

Serves: 4

Recipes

- 1 pound of beef, cubed
- 2 medium-sized onion, diced
- 2 tablespoons of butter
- 4 cups of beef broth
- 2 tablespoons of curry powder
- 2 bay leaves
- 2 big sliced potatoes
- 2 tablespoons of white vinegar
- 1 tablespoon of salt

Direction

Put butter in your pan, let it melt, add beef and onions, and let it simmer until the beef is brown. Then add your beef broth, bay leaves, and curry and let it cook for about 30 minutes.

Then add your potatoes, salt, and vinegar and cook for another 50 minutes. When it is soft, remove it from heat, transfer it to a serving dish and serve hot.

Recipe 18 - Spicy Potato and Mashed Apple

Vegetables are plentiful and combining them with potatoes and apples makes them tasty and very nutritious.

Prep time: 40 minutes

Serves: 6

Recipes

- 2 pounds of rutabaga, peeled and sliced
- 1 big potato, peeled and chopped
- 1 big apple peeled, cored, and chopped
- 1 cup of chicken broth
- 1/2 teaspoon of dried and crumbled thyme
- 1/3 teaspoon of nutmeg
- 1/2 teaspoon of ground cinnamon
- 2 tablespoons of heavy cream

Direction

Mix your potato, rutabaga, apple, thyme, chicken broth, nutmeg, and cinnamon in a large pan and allow to boil. After a while, reduce the heat, cover the pan and let it simmer for another 20 minutes.

Open pan, stir continuously for another 10 minutes, remove and transfer mixture to a bowl. Add the cream and use a food processor to blend the mixture properly until it becomes smooth.

Transfer to a serving dish and serve hot.

Recipe 19 - Creamy Eggplant and Potato Stew

Eggplants with potatoes are a great combination. The eggplant vegetable has always been popular in the south, and it is one of their favorite meal.

Prep time: 40 minutes

Serves: 4

Recipes

- 1/2 cup of bacon grease
- 2 cups of eggplant, diced
- 2 big onions, diced
- 1 cup of celery, diced
- 1 cup of chopped potatoes
- 1 clove of minced garlic
- 1/2 teaspoon of curry powder

- 1/3 teaspoon of dried thyme, crumbled
- 1/3 teaspoon of dried basil, crumbled
- 3 cups of chicken broth
- 1 cup of heavy cream

Direction

Heat your bacon grease in a pan, add your eggplant, celery, onions, garlic, and potatoes, stir and cook for about 15 minutes. Add the thyme, curry powder, and basil and continue cooking until your potatoes are tender and begin to stick to the bottom of the pan.

Add your chicken broth, stir and let it boil. Reduce the heat and continue cooking until the liquid becomes thick. Add your heavy cream, heat a bit, remove and serve.

Recipe 20 - Cheesy Spoonbread

Ever tried eating spoonbread? You indeed love every bit of it. If you are outside your home, now it is time to make it yourself and enjoy the taste with your loved ones.

Prep time: 70 minutes

Serves: 6

Recipes

- 1 can of white cornmeal
- 2 cups of water
- 1/2 tablespoon of salt
- 1/2 cup of cheddar cheese, grated
- 1 cup of milk
- 2 big eggs, whisked
- 1/2 stick of melted butter

Direction

Preheat your oven to about 300°F. Mix the cornmeal in a pan, add water, and salt and let it boil. Reduce heat and allow it to simmer for another 5 minutes while stirring continuously.

Remove pan from heat, add cheese, and stir until it melts. Add your milk, butter, and eggs, mix properly until the mixture is smooth. Transfer mixture to a baking dish, put in your oven, and bake for about 50 minutes or until firm.

Remove from oven and serve hot.

Recipe 21 - Turkey, Beans, and Potato Stew

How do you like your turkey? How about preparing it differently? The southern-styled turkey is prepared with beans and potato to make the stew tasty.

Prep time: 30 minutes
Serves: 4
Recipes

- 4 bacon slices
- 1 big onion, well diced
- 1 well-chopped celery rib
- 1 small green bell pepper, seed removed, and well chopped
- 3 cups of chicken broth
- 1 pack of corn kernels, frozen
- 1 pack of lima beans, frozen

- 2 big potatoes, peeled and cubed
- 2 cups of chopped turkey, chopped
- 1/2 teaspoon of tarragon, dried and crumbled
- 1/2 teaspoon of salt
- 1/2 teaspoon of fresh ground black pepper

Direction

Fry the bacon in a pan until it is crispy, remove and drain on a paper towel and set aside. Add onions, celery, and pepper into the pan and simmer until it is soft. Add your remaining ingredients and bacon into the pan and let it boil.

Cover the pan and cook until the beans are soft, remove from heat and serve hot.

Recipe 22 - Baked Potatoes and Pineapple

Spicy baked potatoes seasoned with crumbled pineapple will make your taste bud dance for joy. What makes it tastier is that you have to make it yourself and just the way you love it.

Prep time: 60 minutes

Serves: 4

Recipes

- 4 medium-sized sweet potatoes
- 1 cup of milk
- 1⁄2 cup of sugar
- 1⁄4 cup of canned pineapple, crushed
- 1/2 stick of butter
- 2 large eggs, whisked
- 1⁄4 teaspoon of salt

- 1/3 teaspoon of ground cinnamon
- 1/2 cup of flaked unsweetened coconut, packaged

Direction

Preheat your oven to about 360°F. Put your potatoes in a pan, add water and cook until they are soft. Remove from pan, drain and allow to cool. When you can manage it, peel it and place it in a bowl. Using a fork, mash it properly.

Add your remaining ingredients to the mashed potatoes except for the flaked coconut. Keep mashing until it is well mixed and smooth. Transfer mixture into a baking dish and bake for about 40 minutes.

Remove from oven, sprinkle your coconut flakes on it, and serve hot.

Recipe 23 - Spicy Catfish Stew

Like all other types of fish, catfish are very healthy and nutritious, and you will undoubtedly enjoy this catfish stew with something on the side.

Prep time: 40 minutes
Serves: 4
Recipes

- 5 bacon slices, chopped in cubes
- 2 medium-sized onions, finely diced
- 3 large tomatoes, chopped
- 2 big potatoes, peeled and cubed
- 2 cups of water
- 1/2 teaspoon of ground cloves
- 2 tablespoons of Worcestershire sauce

- 1 teaspoon of Tabasco sauce
- 1 teaspoon of salt
- 1 teaspoon of fresh ground black pepper
- 2 pounds of catfish fillets, cut

Direction

Fry the bacon in a pan until crispy, remove and drain on a paper towel and set aside. Ass the onions to the pan, simmer until it is soft. Add the potatoes, tomatoes, cloves, water, Tabasco, and Worcestershire sauce. Add your salt and pepper also, stir and allow it to boil for at least 30 minutes.

Add the catfish and bacon, stir and cover the pan and cook until the fish is well cooked. Remove and serve hot.

Recipe 24 - Spicy Butter Beans and Peas

The southern Africans are a lover of peas, no matter the type or shape of the peas. Combining the peas with fresh butter beans and a little seasoning gives a very healthy and nutritious meal.

Prep time: 30 minutes

Serves: 6

Recipes

- 2 cups of fresh crowder peas, fresh
- 2 cups of fresh butter beans, shelled
- 2 pounds of diced pork
- 1 medium-sized hot red pepper, seed removed and diced
- 1 teaspoon of salt
- 1 teaspoon of ground black pepper

- 1 small red onion, diced

Direction

Place your peas and beans in a bowl of water, rinse, remove and discard any particles. Transfer to a pan, add the pork, salt, red pepper, and ground pepper. Add water and let it boil until they are soft.

Drain the peas and beans, transfer to a serving dish, sprinkle onions on it, and serve hot.

Recipe 25 - Fried Chicken Dipped in Beer

The cooks in the south have always loved fried chicken with a little fermented beer to make it tastier.

Prep time: 60 minutes

Serves: 2

Recipes

- 2 cups of flour
- 3 pounds of lager beer
- 1/2 teaspoon of salt
- 1/2 teaspoon of Tabasco sauce
- 1 cup of vegetable shortening
- 3 pounds of chicken, chopped

Direction

Mix the flour, salt, beer, and Tabasco in a bowl and mix until it is very smooth and let it stand for about 50 minutes. Pour the shortening into a frying pan, dip your chicken in your beer mixture and fry until it becomes golden brown.

Remove from pan, drain, and serve warm.

Recipe 26 - Baked Beans Mixed with Ketchup and Coca-Cola

This is one of a kind meal and can mostly be found in southern Africa restaurant. You might be used to making puddings with beverages, but this meal is unique and tastes excellent with Coca-Cola.

Prep time: 70 minutes

Serves: 5

Recipes

- 1 tablespoon dried mustard
- 2 cans baked beans mixed with pork
- 1 medium-sized onion, finely diced
- 1/2 cup ketchup
- 1/2 cup Coca-Cola
- 1 teaspoon salt
- 1 cup of brown sugar

- 1 teaspoon fresh ground black pepper
- 5 bacon slices

Direction

Preheat your oven to about 300°F. Mix your baked beans, sugar, onions, coke, ketchup, mustard, salt, and pepper in a bowl, mix well and transfer the mixture to a baking dish.

Place your bacon on it and bake for about 60 minutes or until your beans begin to bubble and the bacon is well cooked. Remove from oven and serve hot.

Recipe 27 - Chicken in Orange and Curry

This long-age recipe has been in existence in the south for years, and it hasn't lost that unique taste until now. You don't need to travel to the south to have it; all you need is to get the ingredients and enjoy the meal.

Prep time: 60 minutes

Serves: 3

Recipes

- 3 chicken breast, split
- 2 tablespoons of butter, chopped
- 1 teaspoon of salt
- 1/2 teaspoon of fresh ground black pepper
- 2 cups of orange juice
- 1/2 cup of dark raisins

- 1/2 cup of almonds, chopped
- 1/3 tablespoon of curry powder
- 1/2 teaspoon of crumbled dried thyme
- 1/3 cup of fresh parsley, chopped

Direction

Preheat your oven to about 400°F. Arrange your chicken in a shallow and grease baking pan, scatter your butter on it, season it with a bit of salt and pepper, put it in your oven, and bake for about 20 minutes.

Mix the raisins, juice, almonds, curry, and thyme in a pan and boil for about 10 minutes. Pour the mixture on the chicken and bake for another 30 minutes or until your chicken is tender.

Remove and serve.

Recipe 28 - Lemon Flavored Swordfish Barbeque

Swordfish is a fantastic fish because of its firm and meaty nature. It is one of the best fish to use for a barbeque for the fat family get-together you are planning during summer.

Prep time: 70 minutes

Serves: 6

Recipes

- 4 pounds of swordfish steaks, fresh and center cut
- 1/3 cup of dry rub barbeque mix
- 2 tablespoons of oil
- 1/2 stick of melted butter
- 1/2 cup of lemon wedges

Direction

Season your swordfish with the barbeque rub, cover the dish with plastic wrap and let it rest for about 25 minutes. Light your charcoal grill and let it burn for about 30 minutes.

Place your grill rack several inches away from the flame, brush it with your oil, and place the fish steak on it. Brush the fish with your butter, grill for 5 minutes or until your fish is flaked.

Brush with butter again, remove and serve with lemon wedges and juice squeezed from it.

Recipe 29 - Baked Crab Meat

Baked crab meat is one of the simplest dishes that the southern African has. The sauce and sherry are used in preparing to give a unique taste.

Prep time: 30 minutes

Serves: 4

Recipes

- 2 pounds of crabmeat, shell removed
- 2 tablespoons of vinegar
- 1 tablespoon of sweet sherry
- 1/2 stick of melted butter
- 1 teaspoon of Worcestershire sauce
- 1/3 cup of fresh chives, minced
- 1 teaspoon of salt

- 1/2 teaspoon of fresh ground black pepper
- 1/2 cup of Tabasco sauce

Direction

Preheat your oven to about 300°F. Mix all ingredients in a bowl, divide the mixture into 4 separate oval-shaped pans.

Put in your oven and bake for about 20 minutes or until it begins to bubble. Remove and serve hot.

Recipe 30 - Crabs Wrapped in Mustard Seeds

When most travelers visit Southern Africa, they don't mind waiting long hours in the restaurant just to have this special crab meal.

Prep time: 10 minutes

Serves: 4

Recipes

- 2 tablespoons of mustard, dried
- 1 can of mayonnaise
- 1/2 cup of half and half
- 1/2 tablespoon of Worcestershire sauce
- 1 teaspoon of steak sauce
- 1 teaspoon of salt

Direction

Mix all the ingredients in a bowl and mix properly with a mixer for about 5 minutes or until it is creamy. Cover with foil, place in your refrigerator, and chill before you serve.

Conclusion

Southern Africa is a beautiful place to behold. And not only are the cities in it beautiful, but they also have many amazing meals that you need to try. This cookbook is a combination of the finest and most tasty Southern Africa recipes that will suit your taste bud.

Don't miss out!

Visit the website below and you can sign up to receive emails whenever Ida Smith publishes a new book. There's no charge and no obligation.

https://books2read.com/r/B-A-LRXL-IZGRB

BOOKS 2 READ

Connecting independent readers to independent writers.

Did you love *Take A Trip Around Southern Recipes: Around Southern Africa with 30 Unique Recipes*? Then you should read *Street Food African - Savoring the goodness of the plains: Tasting your way across the plains*[1] by Ida Smith!

[2]

Street food is how to taste the rich flavors of Africa, meet the locals, and a meeting point for discussing the issues that plague the continent. African food is delicious and cooked for all who desire to eat something different and fulfilling. So, if you have never been to Africa, you should try to visit just to taste the food.

---

1. https://books2read.com/u/m2Mnjr

2. https://books2read.com/u/m2Mnjr